Songbook

Authors

Lynn M. Brinckmeyer Texas State University, San Marcos, Texas

Amy M. Burns Far Hills Country Day School, Far Hills, New Jersey

Patricia Shehan Campbell University of Washington, Seattle, Washington

Audrey Cardany University of Rhode Island, Kingston, Rhode Island

Shelly Cooper University of Nebraska at Omaha, Omaha, Nebraska

Anne M. Fennell Vista Unified School District, Vista, California

Sanna Longden Clinician/Consultant, Evanston, Illinois

Rochelle G. Mann Fort Lewis College, Durango, Colorado

Nan L. McDonald San Diego State University, San Diego, California

Martina Miranda University of Colorado, Boulder, Colorado

Sandra L. Stauffer Arizona State University, Tempe, Arizona

Phyllis Thomas Lewisville Independent School District, Lewisville, Texas

Charles Tighe Cobb County School District, Atlanta, Georgia

Maribeth Yoder-White Clinician/Consultant, Banner Elk, North Carolina

 in partnership with

Boston, Massachusetts
Chandler, Arizona
Glenview, Illinois
New York, New York

interactive MUSIC powered by Silver Burdett™ with Alfred Music Publishing Co., Inc.

ISBN-13: 978-1-4182-6265-5
ISBN-10:   1-4182-6265-X
9 19

A la rurru niño
(Hush, My Little Baby)

Folk Song from Mexico
English Words by Verne Muñoz

A la ru - rru ni - ño,
Hush, my lit - tle ba - by,

A la ru - rru ya,___
Close your sleep - y eyes;___

Duér - me - te, mi ni - ño,
I will sing a song for you,

Y duér - me - te ya.___
Lul - la, lul - la - by.___

The Alphabet Song

Traditional Song
Based on a Folk Melody from France

Andy Pandy

Traditional

1. An - dy Pan - dy, fine and dan - dy, All pop down.
2. An - dy Pan - dy, fine and dan - dy, All pop up.
3. An - dy Pan - dy, fine and dan - dy, All pop in.
4. An - dy Pan - dy, fine and dan - dy, All pop out.

Bluebird, Bluebird

Game Song from the United States

1. Blue - bird, blue - bird through my win - dow,
2. Take a little girl and tap her on the should - er,
3. Take a little boy and tap him on the should - er,

Blue - bird, blue - bird through my win - dow,
Take a little girl and tap her on the should - er,
Take a little boy and tap him on the should - er,

Blue - bird, blue - bird through my win - dow,
Take a little girl and tap her on the should - er,
Take a little boy and tap him on the should - er,

Oh, John - ny, I am tired.

The Bus

Traditional

1. The peo-ple in the bus go up and down,
2. The wheels on the bus go 'round and 'round,
3. The horn on the bus goes, "Beep, beep, beep,
4. The mon-ey in the box goes, "Clink, clink, clink,

Up and down, up and down.
'Round and 'round, 'round and 'round.
Beep, beep, beep, beep, beep, beep!"
Clink, clink, clink, clink, clink, clink!"

The peo-ple in the bus go up and down,
The wheels on the bus go 'round and 'round,
The horn on the bus goes, "Beep, beep, beep!"
The mon-ey in the box goes, "Clink, clink, clink!"

All a - round the town.

5. The wipers on the bus go, "Swish, swish, swish,
   Swish, swish, swish, swish, swish, swish!"
   The wipers on the bus go, "Swish, swish, swish!"
   All around the town.

6. The driver on the bus says, "Move on back,
   Move on back, move on back!"
   The driver on the bus says, "Move on back!"
   All around the town.

Cha yang wu
(Rice Planting Song)

Folk Song from China
Words Adapted by Patricia Shehan Campbell

do—

Tai   yang   he   na   nuan   fung   chui;
Sun   shines   bright,   warm   breez - es   blow,

Miao   er   jang   duh   fei   yu   mei,
Ti - ny   plants   of   rice   will   grow.

Da   jia   tien   li   cha   yang   miao:
Ev - 'ry   one   will   rake   and   hoe.

E   hang,   e   hang,   kwai   yu   fei;
Plow - ing,   plant - ing   row   by   row.

Hai,   hai,   huh,   Hai,   hai,   ho,
Hai,   hai,   huh,   Hai,   hai,   ho,

Cha   hao   miao   er   jang   gu   na.
Plant - ing   rice   is   ver - y   nice.

Chippewa Lullaby

Native American Song of the Chippewa People
Collected by Frances Densmore, 1913

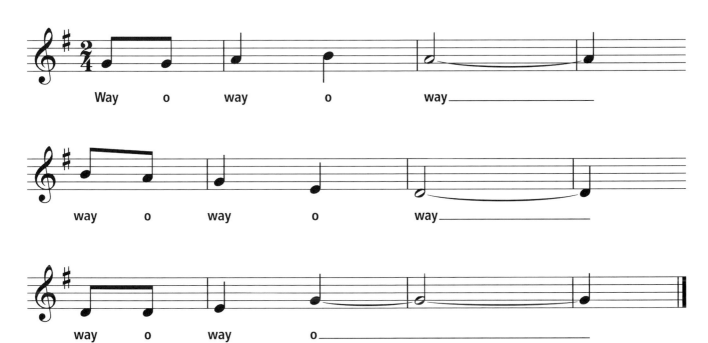

Way   o   way   o   way

way   o   way   o   way

way   o   way   o

Clouds

*Words and Music by Georgia Garlid
and Lynn Freeman Olson*

Cobbler, Cobbler

Traditional
Arranged by Michael Story

1. Cob - bler, cob - bler, mend my shoe, have it done by half past two;
2. Cob - bler, cob - bler, mend my shoe. Yes, good doc - tor, that I'll do.

half past two is much too late, have it done by half past eight.
Stitch it up and stitch it down, I will charge you one half crown.

Corn Grinding Song

Native American Folk Melody of the Hopi People
Collected by Frank Hamilton Cushing
English Words Traditional

Grind - ing corn, grind - ing corn, Here we are grind - ing corn.

Grains of red and yel - low, blue and white corn I am grind - ing.

Dinner Music

Work Song from the Congo (Zaire)
Collected by Roberta McLaughlin
Words Adapted by Patricia Shehan Campbell

Solo   *Chorus*

First we go to pick from our gar - den, ya, ya, we do.

Solo   *Chorus*

Next we car - ry jugs of wa - ter, ya, ya, we do.

Solo

Then we mash the yel - low corn and cook all day from ear - ly morn.

Solo   *Chorus*

Now we eat, let's gath - er 'round to - geth - er, ya, ya, we do.

Do, Re, Mi Tapping Song

Words and Music by
Christine H. Barden

do— I can tap my knees. I can tap my knees. I can call it *do, do, do*. I can

call it *do, do, do*. I can tap my tum-my. I can tap my tum-my. I can

call it *re, re, re*. I can call it *re, re, re*. I can tap my chest. I can

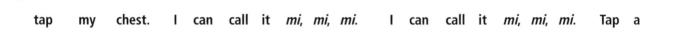

tap my chest. I can call it *mi, mi, mi*. I can call it *mi, mi, mi*. Tap a

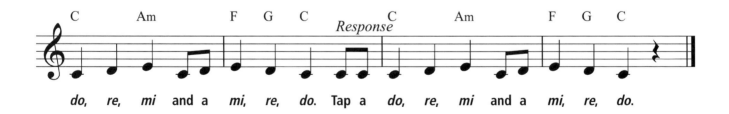

do, re, mi and a *mi, re, do*. Tap a *do, re, mi* and a *mi, re, do*.

Do Your Ears Hang Low?*

Arranged by E.L. Lancaster
Additional Words by Christine H. Barden

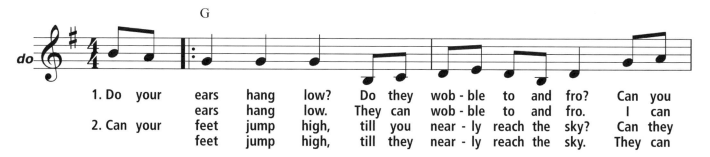

1. Do your ears hang low? Do they wob-ble to and fro? Can you
ears hang low. They can wob-ble to and fro. I can
2. Can your feet jump high, till you near-ly reach the sky? Can they
feet jump high, till they near-ly reach the sky. They can

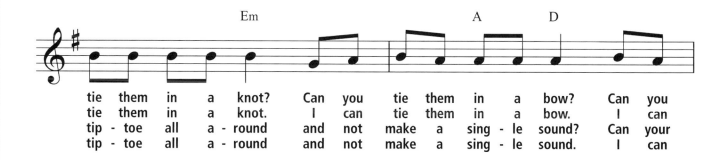

tie them in a knot? Can you tie them in a bow? Can you
tie them in a knot. I can tie them in a bow. I can
tip-toe all a-round and not make a sing-le sound? Can your
tip-toe all a-round and not make a sing-le sound. I can

Last time To Coda ⊕

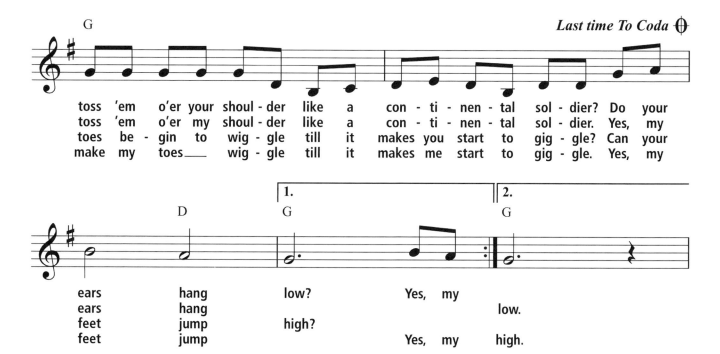

toss 'em o'er your shoul-der like a con-ti-nen-tal sol-dier? Do your
toss 'em o'er my shoul-der like a con-ti-nen-tal sol-dier. Yes, my
toes be-gin to wig-gle till it makes you start to gig-gle? Can your
make my toes___ wig-gle till it makes me start to gig-gle. Yes, my

1.
ears hang low? Yes, my
ears hang
feet jump high?
feet jump

2.
ears hang low.
feet jump Yes, my high.

*includes a verse from "Turkey in the Straw"

Do Your Ears Hang Low?

G   G/F♯   Em7   G/D   C   C/B

Teacher   *Children*   *Teacher*

Tur - key in the straw,   tur - key in the straw,   tur - key in the hay,

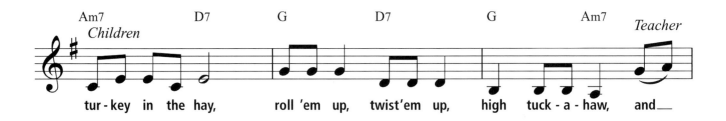

Am7   D7   G   D7   G   Am7

Children   *Teacher*

tur - key in the hay,   roll 'em up, twist 'em up,   high tuck - a - haw, and___

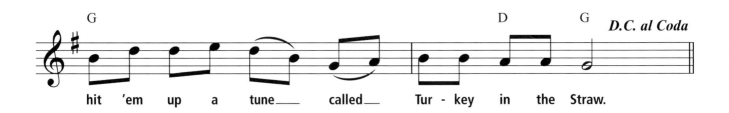

G   D   G   ***D.C. al Coda***

hit 'em up a tune___ called___ Tur - key in the Straw.

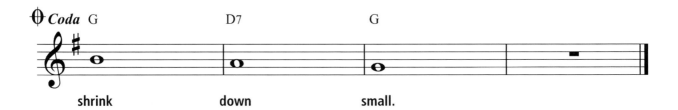

✛ ***Coda*** G   D7   G

shrink   down   small.

3. Can you shrink down small,
so we can't see you at all?
Till you're smaller than a bug
that is sitting on a rug?
Can you sit so quietly
that we'll think you are asleep?
Can you shrink down small?

I can shrink down small,
so you can't see me at all.
Till I'm smaller than a bug
that is sitting on a rug.
I can sit so quietly
that you'll think I am asleep.
I can shrink down small.

Down in the Meadow

Folk Song from the United States

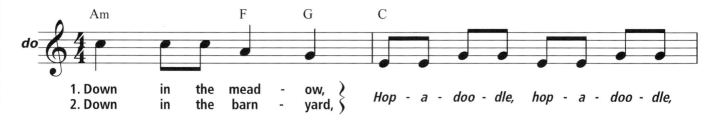

1. Down in the mead - ow, } Hop - a - doo - dle, hop - a - doo - dle,
2. Down in the barn - yard, }

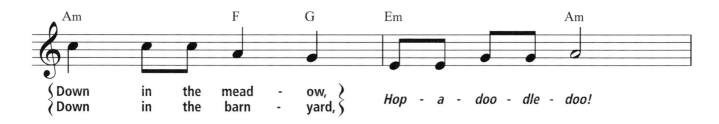

{ Down in the mead - ow, } Hop - a - doo - dle - doo!
{ Down in the barn - yard, }

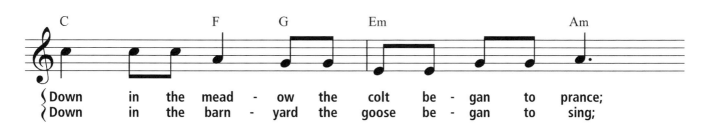

{ Down in the mead - ow the colt be - gan to prance;
{ Down in the barn - yard the goose be - gan to sing;

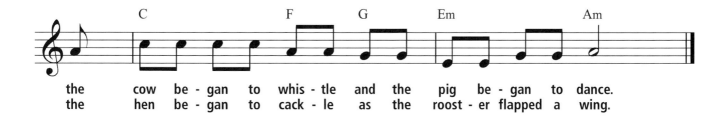

the cow be - gan to whis - tle and the pig be - gan to dance.
the hen be - gan to cack - le as the roost - er flapped a wing.

Down in the Meadow

Make the sounds the animals make in the song.

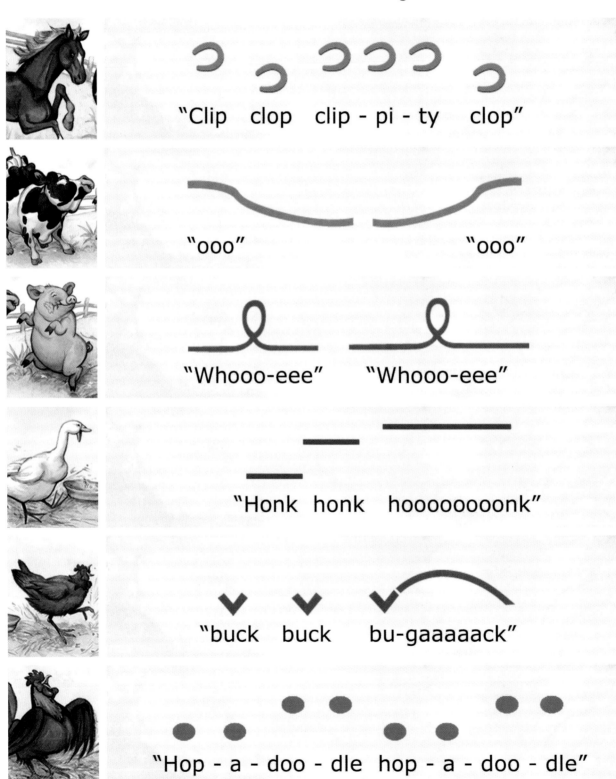

"Clip   clop   clip - pi - ty   clop"

"ooo"   "ooo"

"Whooo-eee"   "Whooo-eee"

"Honk   honk   hooooooonk"

"buck   buck   bu-gaaaaack"

"Hop - a - doo - dle hop - a - doo - dle"

Ee jer ha ba go
(The Hungry Dog)

Children's Song from China
Collected by Mary Shamrock
English Words by Will Gau

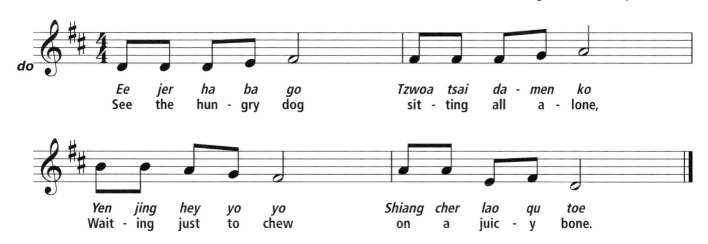

do

Ee jer ha ba go   Tzwoa tsai da - men ko
See the hun - gry dog   sit - ting all a - lone,

Yen jing hey yo yo   Shiang cher lao qu toe
Wait - ing just to chew   on a juic - y bone.

Eensy Weensy Spider

Traditional Children's Song of the United States

Ég a gyertya
(Candle Burning Bright)

Children's Song from Hungary
English Words by Rochelle Mann

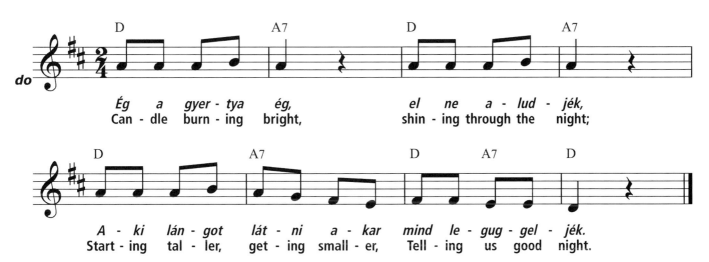

do

Ég a gyer - tya ég, el ne a - lud - jék,
Can - dle burn - ing bright, shin - ing through the night;

A - ki lán - got lát - ni a - kar mind le - gug - gel - jék.
Start - ing tal - ler, get - ing small - er, Tell - ing us good night.

El caracol
(The Snail's Dance)

Children's Song from Spain
English Words by Sue Ellen LaBelle

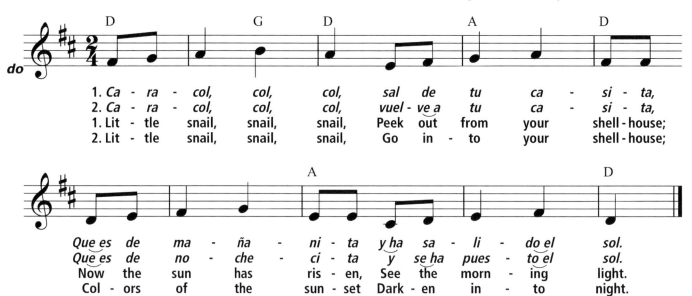

1. Ca - ra - col, col, col, sal de tu ca - si - ta,
2. Ca - ra - col, col, col, vuel - ve a tu ca - si - ta,
1. Lit - tle snail, snail, snail, Peek out from your shell - house;
2. Lit - tle snail, snail, snail, Go in - to your shell - house;

Que es de ma - ña - ni - ta y ha sa - li - do el sol.
Que es de no - che - ci - ta y se ha pues - to el sol.
Now the sun has ris - en, See the morn - ing light.
Col - ors of the sun - set Dark - en in - to night.

Elephant Song

Traditional
Arranged by Michael Story

Playfully

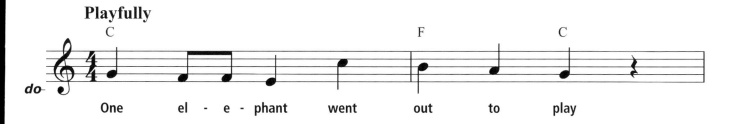

do—

One el - e - phant went out to play

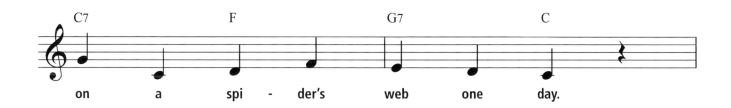

on a spi - der's web one day.

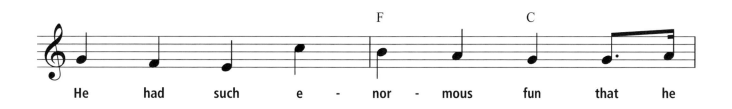

He had such e - nor - mous fun that he

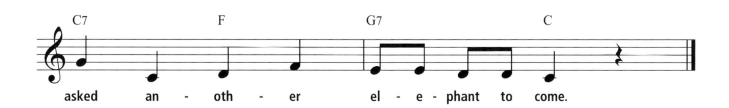

asked an - oth - er el - e - phant to come.

Fais dodo
(Close Your Eyes)

Folk Song from France
English Words by Jean Sinor

do

Fais do - do, 'Co - las, mon p'tit frère,___
Close your eyes and sleep now my broth - er,

Fais do - do, T'au - ras du lo - lo.
Close your eyes; You'll have a sur - prise.

Pa - pa est en bas, il fait du choc' - lat.
Your fa - ther will brew hot cho co - late for you.

Ma - man est en haut, elle fait du gâ - teau.
Your moth - er will bake a won - der - ful cake.

The Farmer in the Dell

Old Singing Game

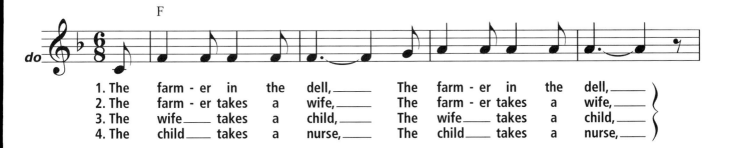

1. The farm - er in the dell, _____ The farm - er in the dell, _____
2. The farm - er takes a wife, _____ The farm - er takes a wife, _____
3. The wife_____ takes a child, _____ The wife_____ takes a child, _____
4. The child_____ takes a nurse, _____ The child_____ takes a nurse, _____

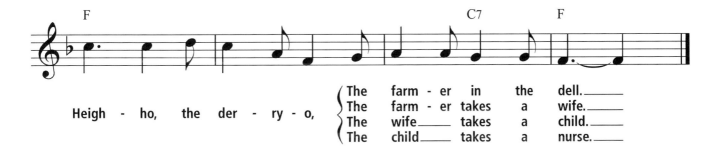

Heigh - ho, the der - ry - o,

The farm - er in the dell. _____
The farm - er takes a wife. _____
The wife_____ takes a child. _____
The child_____ takes a nurse. _____

5. The nurse takes a dog,…

6. The dog takes a cat,…

7. The cat takes a rat,…

8. The rat takes the cheese,…

9. The cheese stands alone,…

Five Little Speckled Frogs

By Virginia Pavelko and Lucille Wood
Arranged by Robert W. Smith

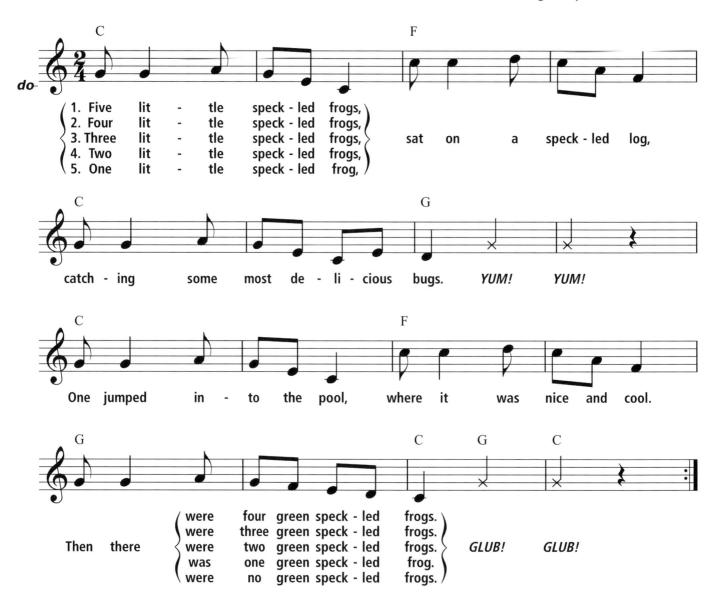

do—

1. Five lit - tle speck - led frogs,
2. Four lit - tle speck - led frogs,
3. Three lit - tle speck - led frogs,
4. Two lit - tle speck - led frogs,
5. One lit - tle speck - led frog,

sat on a speck - led log,

catch - ing some most de - li - cious bugs. *YUM! YUM!*

One jumped in - to the pool, where it was nice and cool.

Then there
were four green speck - led frogs.
were three green speck - led frogs.
were two green speck - led frogs.
was one green speck - led frog.
were no green speck - led frogs.
GLUB! GLUB!

Get on Board

African American Spiritual

Get on board, lit - tle chil - dren, Get on

board, lit - tle chil - dren, Get on board, lit - tle

chil - dren; There's room for man - y - a more.

The gos - pel train's a - com - in', I

hear it close at hand;— I hear the car - wheels

rum - blin' And roll - in' through the land.

Going on a Picnic

*Words and Music by Georgia Garlid
and Lynn Freeman Olson*

Grizzly Bear

Traditional Children's Song

Griz - zly bear, a griz - zly bear is sleep - ing in a cave.

Please be ver - y qui - et, ver - y, ver - y qui - et,

If you wake him, if you shake him, he gets ver - y MAD!

Happy Birthday to You

Words and Music by Mildred J. Hill and Patty S. Hill

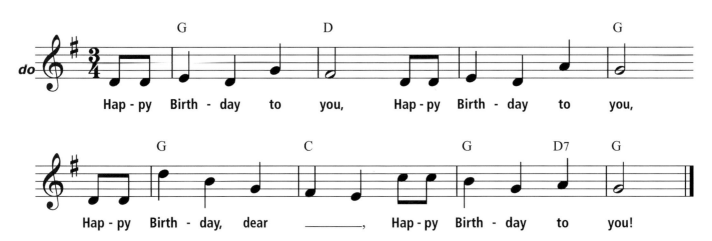

do   Hap - py Birth - day to you,   Hap - py Birth - day to you,

Hap - py Birth - day, dear _____, Hap - py Birth - day to you!

Head and Shoulders

Traditional
Arranged by Christine H. Barden

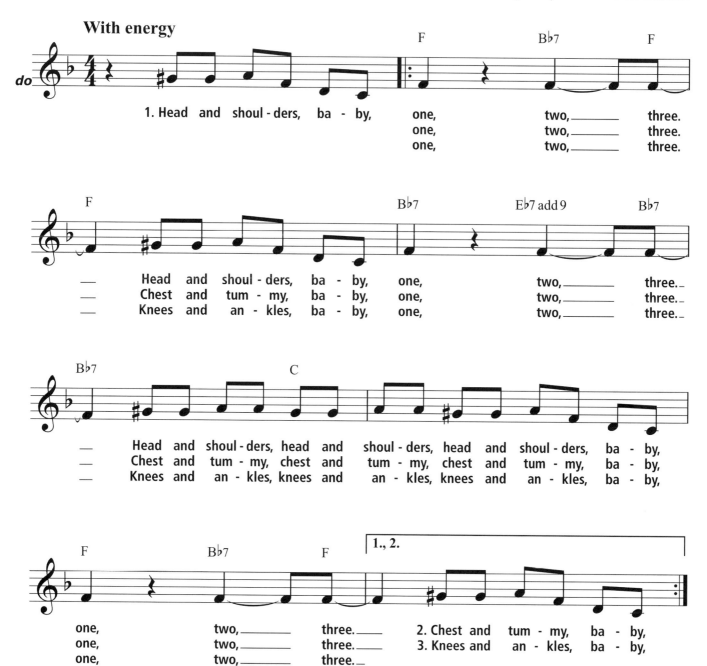

Head and Shoulders

Here We Go 'Round the Mulberry Bush

Traditional
Arranged by Robert W. Smith

1. Here we go 'round the mul - ber - ry bush, the
2. This is the way we wash___ our hands,

mul - ber - ry bush, the mul - ber - ry bush.   Here we go 'round the
wash___ our hands, the mul - ber - ry bush.   This is the way we

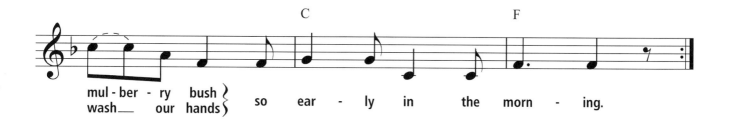

mul - ber - ry bush ⎰ so ear - ly in the morn - ing.
wash___ our hands ⎱

Here We Go 'Round the Mulberry Bush

3. 4. This   is   the   way   we   { go   to   school,
                                    { come   out   of   school,
go   to   school,
come   out   of   school,

go   to   school.}
come   out   of   school.}
This   is   the   way   we   { go   to   school}
                              { come   out   of   school}   so

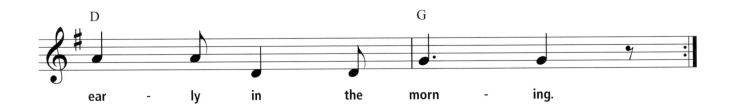

ear   -   ly   in   the   morn   -   ing.

Hey, Hey, Look at Me

Traditional Playground Song
Collected and adapted by Katalin Forrai and Jean Sinor

Hey, hey, look at me, I am {1. smil - ing / 2. sway - ing / 3. bend - ing / 4. nod - ding} you can see.

I'm a Very Fine Turkey

Words and Music by Lillian Wiedman

do—

C   F   C

1. I'm a ver - y fine tur - key and I sing a fine song,
2. And when Thanks - giv - ing Day comes 'round,

C

Gob - ble, gob - ble, gob - ble, gob - ble, gob - ble,
Gob - ble, gob - ble, gob - ble, gob - ble, gob - ble,

C   F   C

I strut a - round the barn - yard all the day long,
I'll go and hide so I can't be found,

F   G7   C

And my head goes bob - ble, bob - ble, bob - ble.
Then my head will still bob - ble as I gob - ble.

I'm Tall, I'm Small

Traditional Children's Song

I'm tall, I'm ver - y tall,

I'm small, I'm ver - y small.

Some - times I'm tall, some - times I'm small.

Guess what I am now.

If You're Happy

Traditional Children's Song of the United States

1. If you're hap-py and you know it, (clap your hands; *(clap, clap)*)
2. tap your foot; *(tap, tap)*
3. nod your head; *(nod, nod)*
4. do all three; *(clap, tap, nod)*

If you're hap-py and you know it, (clap your hands; *(clap, clap)*)
tap your foot; *(tap, tap)*
nod your head; *(nod, nod)*
do all three; *(clap, tap, nod)*

If you're hap-py and you know it, then your face will sure-ly show it;

If you're hap-py and you know it, (clap your hands. *(clap, clap).*)
tap your foot; *(tap, tap).*
nod your head; *(nod, nod).*
do all three; *(clap, tap, nod).*

Ikhanda, maslombe
(My Head and My Shoulders)

Zulu Children's Game Song

I - kha - nda, ma - slo - mbe,
My head and my should - ers,

si - fu - ba, no - kha - lo,
My chest and my mid - dle,

'ma - do - lo, 'na - ma - zwa - ne,
My knees and then my toes, O,

'ma - do - lo, 'na - ma - zwa - ne.
My knees and then my toes, O.

James Brown

African American Game Song
Collected by Patricia Shehan Campbell

James Brown a - walk - ing down the street,

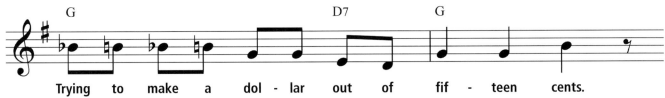

Trying to make a dol - lar out of fif - teen cents.

He missed, he missed, he missed like this, like this, like this.

Jim Along, Josie

Folk Song from Oklahoma

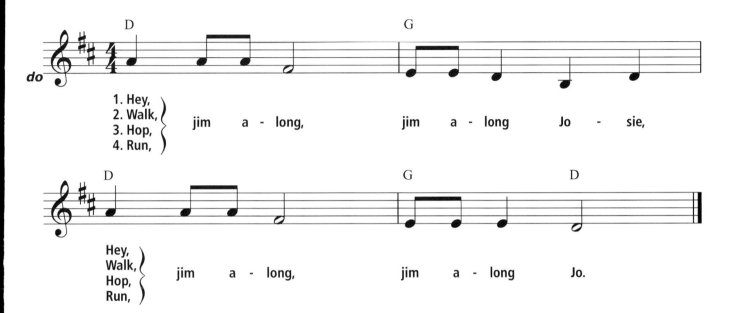

1. Hey,
2. Walk,
3. Hop,
4. Run,
} jim a - long, jim a - long Jo - sie,

Hey,
Walk,
Hop,
Run,
} jim a - long, jim a - long Jo.

5. Jump, jim along,
   jim along Josie,
   Jump, jim along,
   jim along Jo.

6. Tiptoe along,
   jim along Josie,
   Tiptoe along,
   jim along Jo.

7. Crawl along,
   jim along Josie,
   Crawl along,
   jim along Jo.

8. Swing along,
   jim along Josie,
   Swing along,
   jim along Jo.

9. Roll, jim along,
   jim along Josie,
   Roll, jim along,
   jim along Jo.

Jingle Bells

Words and Music by James Pierpont

VERSE

Dash - ing through the snow, In a one - horse o - pen sleigh,

O'er the fields we go, Laugh - ing all the way.

Bells on Bob - tail ring, Mak - ing spir - its bright; What

fun it is to ride and sing A sleigh - ing song to - night! Oh!

Jingle Bells

REFRAIN

F

Jin - gle bells, jin - gle bells, Jin - gle all the way!

B♭   F   G   C7

Oh, what fun it is to ride In a one-horse o - pen sleigh!____

F

Jin - gle bells, jin - gle bells, Jin - gle all the way!

B♭   F   C   C7   F

Oh, what fun it is to ride In a one-horse o - pen sleigh!

Jinny Go 'Round

Folk Song from Missouri

Jin - ny go 'round and a - round and a - round, __

Jin - ny go 'round and a - round and a - round.

Jin - ny go 'round and a - round and a - round,

Way down in Rock - ing - ham.

Johnny Caught a Flea

Folk Song from the United States

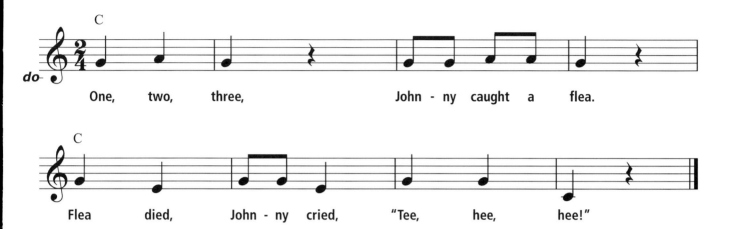

One, two, three, John - ny caught a flea.

Flea died, John - ny cried, "Tee, hee, hee!"

Johnny Mister Brown

African American Children's Song

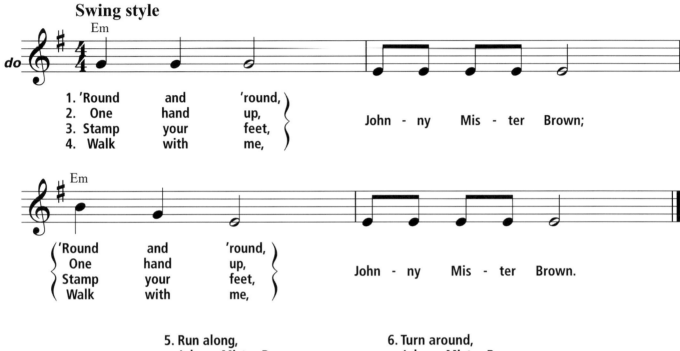

Swing style

Em

do

1. 'Round and 'round,
2. One hand up,
3. Stamp your feet,
4. Walk with me,

John - ny Mis - ter Brown;

Em

'Round and 'round,
One hand up,
Stamp your feet,
Walk with me,

John - ny Mis - ter Brown.

5. Run along,
   Johnny Mister Brown,
   Run along,
   Johnny Mister Brown.

6. Turn around,
   Johnny Mister Brown,
   Turn around,
   Johnny Mister Brown.

44

Johnny Works with One Hammer

Arranged by Christine H. Barden

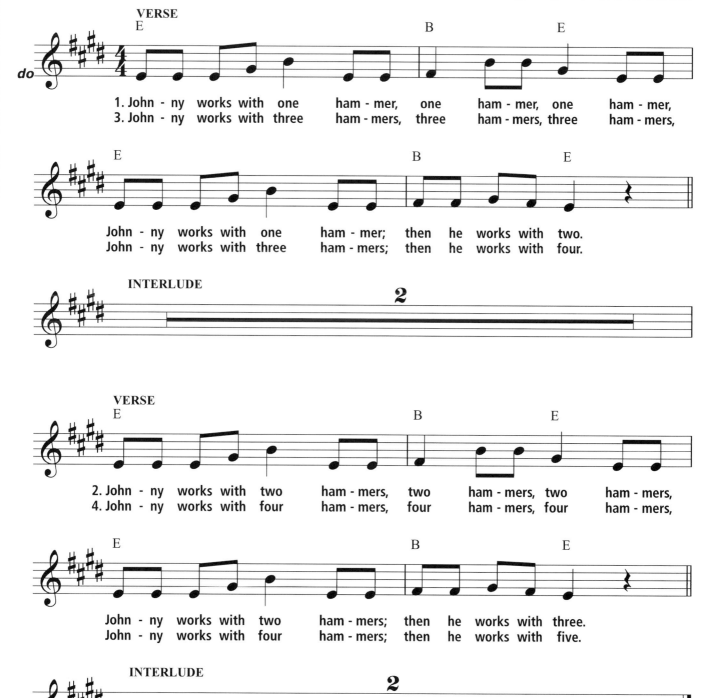

Johnny Works with One Hammer

VERSE

5. John - ny works with five ham - mers, five ham - mers, five ham - mers,

John - ny works with five ham - mers; then he goes to sleep.

Johnny Works with One Hammer

Percussion

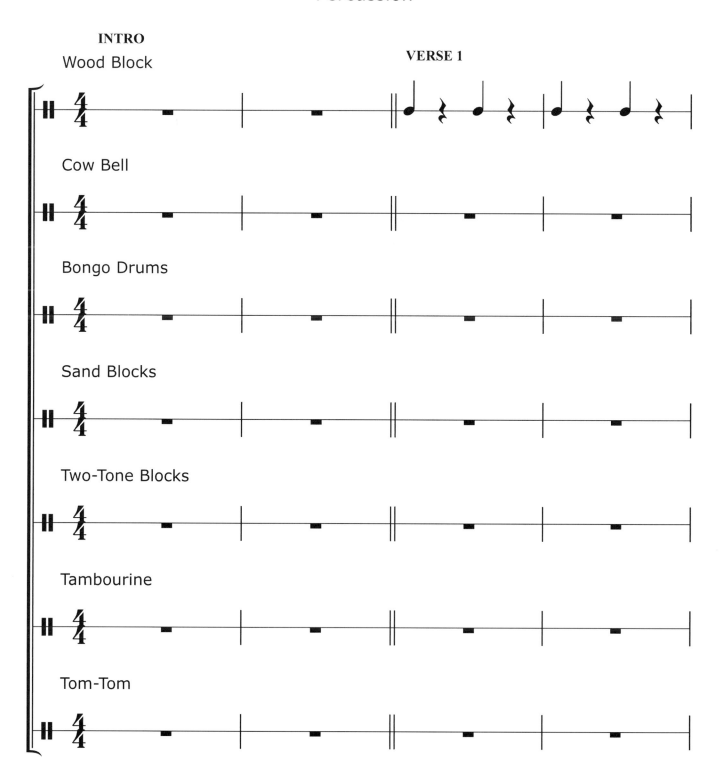

Johnny Works with One Hammer

Johnny Works with One Hammer

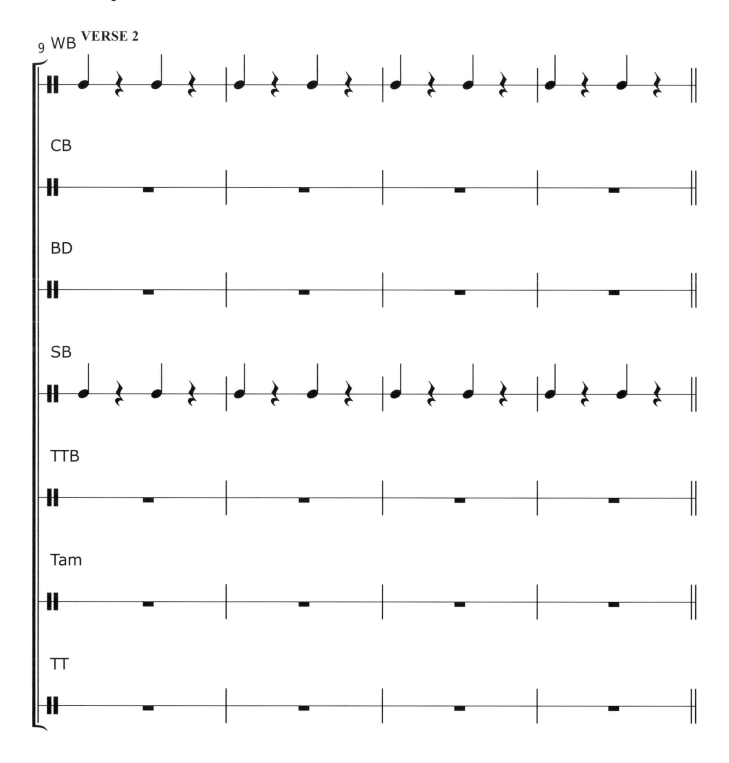

Johnny Works with One Hammer

Johnny Works with One Hammer

Johnny Works with One Hammer

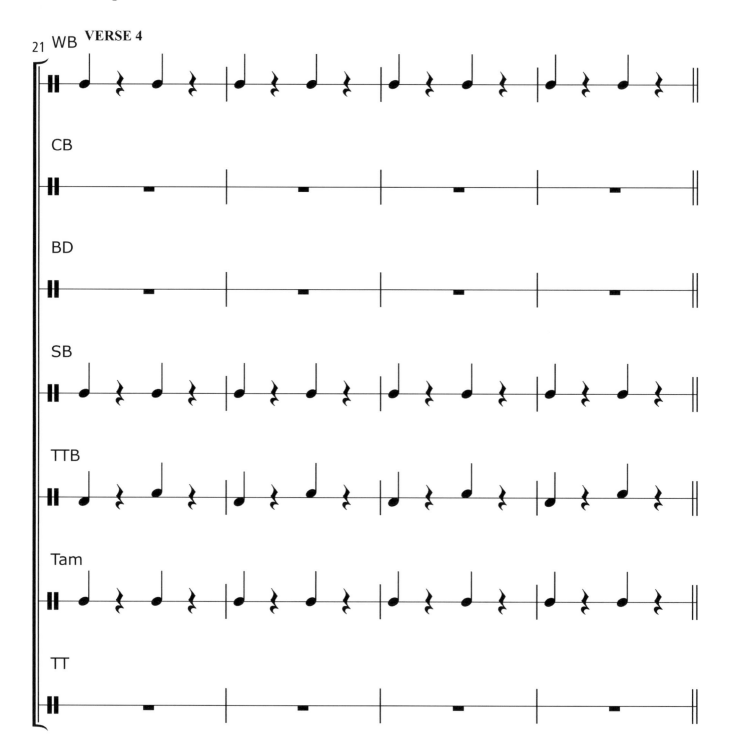

Johnny Works with One Hammer

Johnny Works with One Hammer

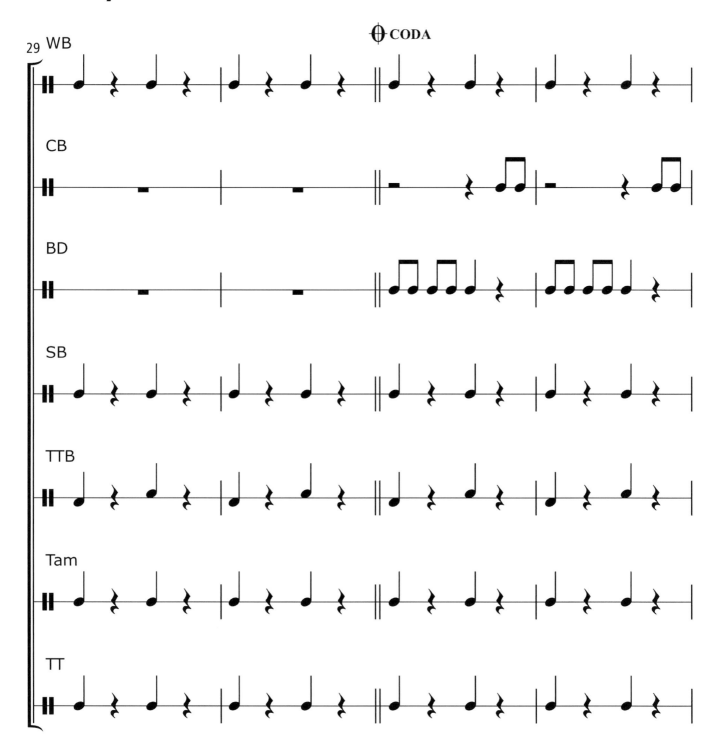

Johnny Works with One Hammer

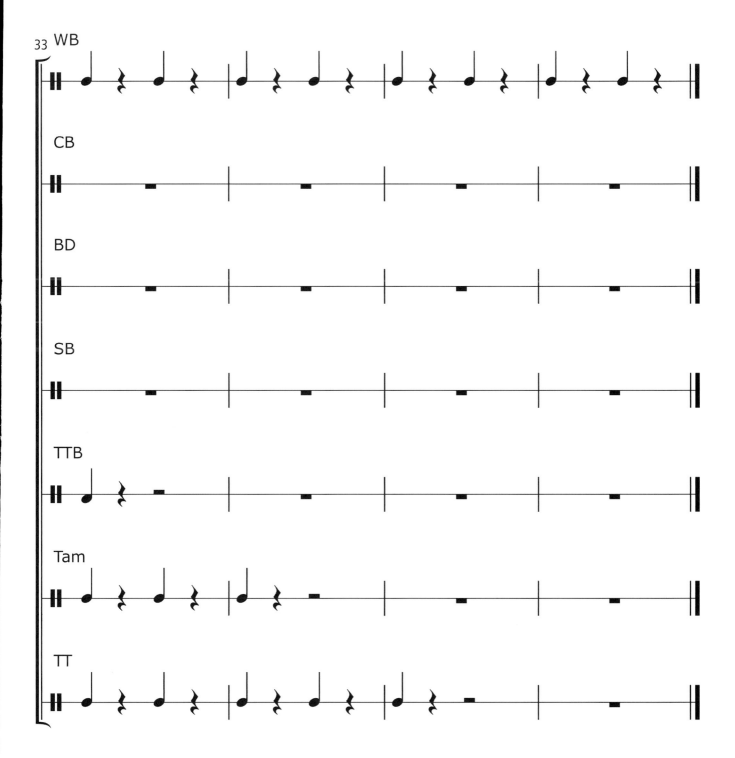

Juan pirulero
(John Lollypop-Seller)

Children's Song from Mexico
English Words by Alice D. Firgau

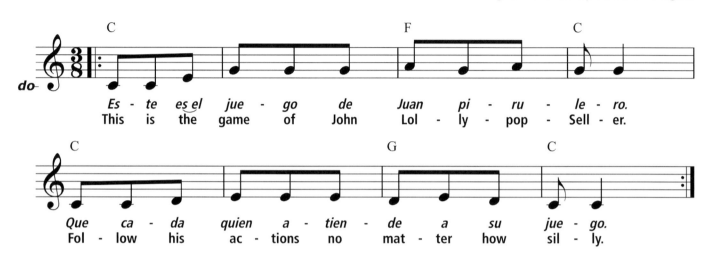

do

Es - te es el jue - go de Juan pi - ru - le - ro.
This is the game of John Lol - ly - pop - Sell - er.

Que ca - da quien a - tien - de a su jue - go.
Fol - low his ac - tions no mat - ter how sil - ly.

Juanito
(Little Johnny)

Children's Song from Spain
English Words by Alice D. Firgau

1., 2. Juan - i - to, cuan - do bai - la, bai - la, bai - la, bai - la;
1., 2. When Lit - tle John - ny danc - es, danc - es, danc - es, danc - es;

Juan - i - to, cuan - do bai - la, bai - la con la ma - no,
                el de - di - to,
When Lit - tle John - ny danc - es, danc - es with his hand,——
                his pink - ie,

Con la ma - no, ma - no, ma - no. ¡Ay qué bien bai - la Juan - i - to!
Con el de - di - to, di - to, di - to.
with his hand,— hand,— hand.— Oh, how smart - ly John - ny danc - es!
with his pink - ie, pink - ie, pink - ie.

3. Juanito, cuando baila,...
 ...con el pie...

4. Juanito, cuando baila,...
 ...con la cabeza...

5. Juanito, cuando baila,...
 ...con el hombro...

6. Juanito, cuando baila,...
 ...con el codo...

3. When Little Johnny dances,...
 ...with his foot...

4. When Little Johnny dances,...
 ...with his head...

5. When Little Johnny dances,...
 ...with his shoulder...

6. When Little Johnny dances,...
 ...with his elbow...

Kaeru no uta
(The Frog Song)

Children's Song from Japan
English Words Courtesy of
CP Language Institute, New York

Ka - e - ru no u - ta ga   Ki - ko - e - te ku - ru - yo
One frog, two frogs, three frogs, hop!   Can you hear their mer - ry song?

Gwa!   Gwa!   Gwa!   Gwa!   Ge-ro, ge-ro, ge-ro, ge-ro, gwa, gwa, gwa!

Kaeru no uta

(The Frog Song)

Percussion

Guiro

Gu

Gu

Gu *(Claps)*

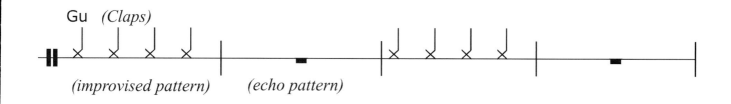

(improvised pattern)   *(echo pattern)*

Gu

Kaeru no uta

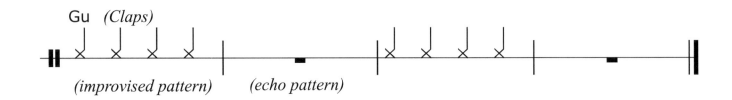

(improvised pattern)   *(echo pattern)*

Koriko!

Children's Marching Song from Senegal, West Africa

Koriko! Ko - ri ko - ri - ko. Koriko! Ko - ri ko - ri - ko.

Ay, yam - ba - la, yam - ba - la ma - ma.

Ay, yam - ba - la, yam - ba - la ma - ma.

Kuma san
(Little Bear)

Children's Rope Skipping Song from the Sendai District, Japan
English Words Courtesy of CP Language Institute, New York

Ku - ma san, Ku - ma san, Ma - wa - re - mi - gi.
Lit - tle Bear, Lit - tle Bear, Turn your - self a - round.

Ku - ma san, Ku - ma san, Ryo te wo tsui te.
Lit - tle Bear, Lit - tle Bear, Now please touch the ground.

Ku - ma san, Ku - ma san, Ka - ta a - shi a - ge te,
Lit - tle Bear, Lit - tle Bear, Jump with just one paw.

Ku - ma san, Ku - ma san, "Sa - yo - na - ra."
Lit - tle Bear, Lit - tle Bear, "Sa - yo - na - ra."

Les petites marionettes
(The Little Marionettes)

Children's Song from France
English Words by Susan Greene

do—

Ain - si font, font, font,
See them dance, dance, dance,

Les pe - ti - tes ma - rio - net - tes,
All the lit - tle mar - io - nettes._____

Ain - si font, font, font,
See them dance, dance, dance,

Trois p'tits tours et puis s'en vont.
Three little turns and off they go!

Little and Lots

Words and Music by Lynn Freeman Olson
and Mary Reilly

do— I love you lit - tle, _____ I love you lots;

My love for you would fill ten pots,

Fif - teen buck - ets, _____ six - teen cans,

Three tea - cups and four dish - pans!

Little Red Wagon

Traditional Song of the United States

1. Rid - ing up and down in the lit - tle red wag - on,
2. Hey!___ What's_ happened to the lit - tle red wag - on?
3. One___ wheel's_ off and the ax - le's drag - gin',
4. Rid - ing up and down in the lit - tle red wag - on,

Rid - ing up and down in the lit - tle red wag - on,
Hey!___ What's_ happened to the lit - tle red wag - on?
One___ wheel's_ off and the ax - le's drag - gin',
Rid - ing up and down in the lit - tle red wag - on,

Rid - ing up and down in the lit - tle red wag - on,
Hey!___ What's_ happened to the lit - tle red wag - on?
One___ wheel's_ off and the ax - le's drag - gin',
Rid - ing up and down in the lit - tle red wag - on,

Won't you be my dar - ling?

Little Red Wagon

Play this accompaniment for "Little Red Wagon."

Little Spider

Hungarian Folk Melody: "Csiga-biga"
New English Words by Jean Sinor

Lit - tle spi - der spins all day,

Spins while all the oth - ers play.

Then the web is fin - 'ly done,

Shin - ing in the morn - ing sun.

London Bridge

Singing Game from England

1. Lon - don Bridge is fall - ing down,   fall - ing down,   fall - ing down,
2. Build   it   up   with   i - ron   bars,   i - ron   bars,   i - ron   bars,
3. I - ron bars will bend and break,   bend and break,   bend and break,
4. Build   it   up   with silver and gold,   silver and gold,   silver and gold,

Lon - don Bridge is fall - ing down,
Build   it   up   with   i - ron   bars,
I - ron bars will bend and break,
Build   it   up   with silver and gold,

my   fair   la - dy.

Looby Loo

Traditional Song of the United States and England

Energetically

REFRAIN

Here we dance loo - by loo, ____ Here we dance loo - by light, ____

Here we dance loo - by loo, ____ All on a Sat - ur - day night. ____

VERSE

I put my
{
1. right hand
2. left hand
3. right foot
4. left foot
}
in, ____ I put my
{
right hand
left hand
right foot
left foot
}
out, ____

I give my
{
right hand
left hand
right foot
left foot
}
a shake, shake, shake, And turn my - self a - bout. ____

5. I put my whole self in,
   I put my whole self out,
   I give my whole self a shake, shake, shake,
   And turn myself about.

Mary Came a-Running

African American Game Song of the Georgia Environs

5. Friday morning...

6. Saturday morning...

7. Sunday morning...

Mary Wore Her Red Dress

Folk Song of the United States

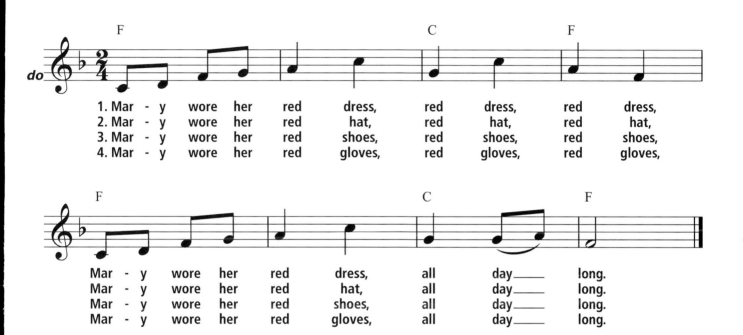

do

1. Mar - y wore her red dress, red dress, red dress,
2. Mar - y wore her red hat, red hat, red hat,
3. Mar - y wore her red shoes, red shoes, red shoes,
4. Mar - y wore her red gloves, red gloves, red gloves,

Mar - y wore her red dress, all day___ long.
Mar - y wore her red hat, all day___ long.
Mar - y wore her red shoes, all day___ long.
Mar - y wore her red gloves, all day___ long.

5. Mary was a red bird, red bird, red bird,
   Mary was a red bird, all day long.

Mbombera

Folk Song from Zimbabwe
As sung by Dumisani Maraire

Mbom - be - ra, Mbom - be - ra ye sti - me - la.

Ne - na ne na na, Ne - na ne na na,

Ne - na ne na na, Na - na na na na.

Mi cuerpo hace música
(There's Music in Me)

Folk Song from Puerto Rico
English Words by David Eddleman

REFRAIN

Mi cuer - po,___ mi cuer - po___ ha - ce mú - si - ca. Mi
There's mu - sic,___ there's mu - sic___ right in - side of me. There's

cuer - po,___ mi cuer - po___ ha - ce mú - si - ca. Mi
mu - sic,___ there's mu - sic___ right in - side of___ me. My

VERSE

bo - ca ha - ce la, la, la. Mis ma - nos ha - cen
mouth can go la, la, la, la. And both my hands can

(clap, clap, clap) Mis pies ha - cen ta, ta, ta. Mi cin - tu - ra ha - ce
(clap, clap, clap) My feet, they go tap, tap, tap. And my hips can dance the

Cha, cha, cha. Cha, cha, cha. Mi cin - tu - ra ha - ce cha, cha, cha.
Cha, cha, cha. Cha, cha, cha. And my hips can dance the cha, cha, cha.

Cha, cha, cha. Mi cin - tu - ra ha - ce cha, cha, cha.
Cha, cha, cha. And my hips can dance the cha, cha, cha.

73

Mi cuerpo hace música
(There's Music in Me)
Percussion

Miss Susie Anna Sue

African American Game Song
Collected by John W. Work

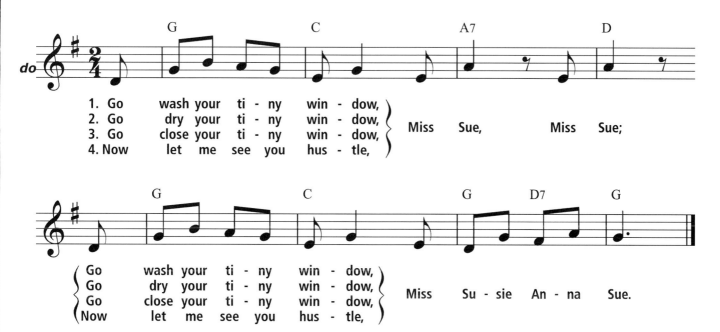

1. Go   wash your ti - ny win - dow,
2. Go   dry your ti - ny win - dow,
3. Go   close your ti - ny win - dow,
4. Now   let me see you hus - tle,

Miss   Sue,   Miss   Sue;

Go   wash your ti - ny win - dow,
Go   dry your ti - ny win - dow,
Go   close your ti - ny win - dow,
Now   let me see you hus - tle,

Miss   Su - sie An - na Sue.

Mon son pha
(Mon Hides the Cloth)

Mon Rhyme from Western Thailand
English Words by Sue Ellen LaBelle

Mon son pha tuk - ka - ta yu kang lung wai
Where will Mon hide the cloth? O - ver here! Tell

non wai ni chan cha ti kon thoe
me where! Look be - hind his back! Whack!

Muffin Man

Traditional
Arranged by Robert W. Smith

Do you know the muf - fin man, the muf - fin man, the muf - fin man?

Oh, do you know the muf - fin man who lives on Dru - ry Lane?

Muffin Man

Percussion

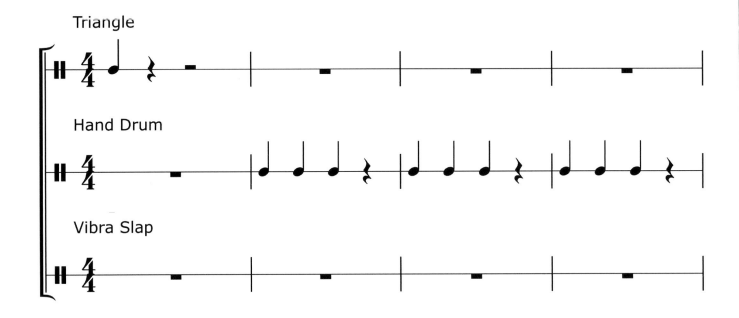

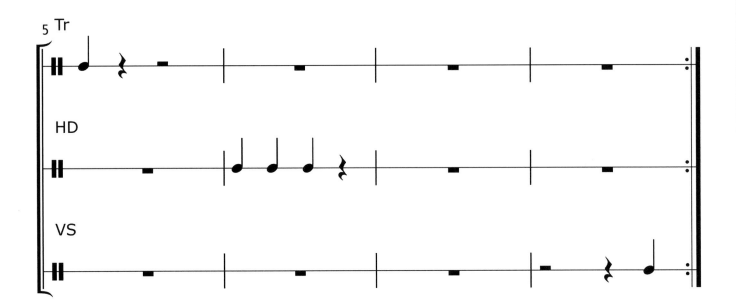

My Valentine

Music by Ruth Stephens Porter
Words by Frank Hagerman

1. Will you be my val - en - tine, val - en - tine, val - en - tine?
2. Yes, I'll be your val - en - tine, val - en - tine, val - en - tine.

Will you be my val - en - tine? I love you.
Yes, I'll be your val - en - tine. I love you.

Nanny Goat

Children's Song from Jamaica

1. Hop on one foot,
2. Clap your hands now,
3. Tap your knees now,
4. Stamp your feet now,

Nan - ny Goat, Nan - ny Goat;

Hop on one foot,
Clap your hands now,
Tap your knees now,
Stamp your feet now,

Nan - ny Goat; do!

Hop on one foot,
Clap your hands now,
Tap your knees now,
Stamp your feet now,

Nan - ny Goat, Nan - ny Goat;

Hop on one foot,
Clap your hands now,
Tap your knees now,
Stamp your feet now,

Nan - ny Goat, do!

5. Do what I do,...

O ma washi

(Go Around the Cat's Eye)

Folk Song from Japan

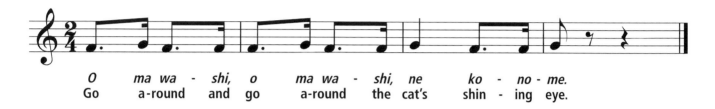

O ma wa - shi, o ma wa - shi, ne ko - no - me.
Go a-round and go a-round the cat's shin - ing eye.

The Old Gray Cat

Traditional
Arranged by Christine H. Barden

Sleeping peacefully

The old gray cat is sleep - ing, sleep - ing,

sleep - ing. The old gray cat is sleep - ing in the house.

The

Cautiously creeping

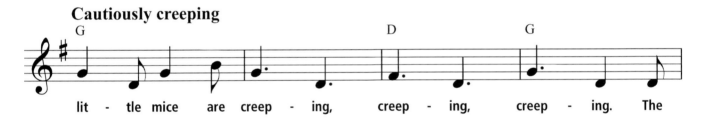

lit - tle mice are creep - ing, creep - ing, creep - ing. The

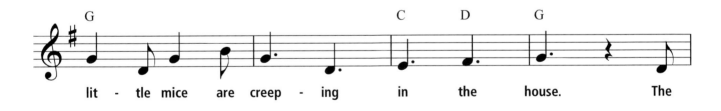

lit - tle mice are creep - ing in the house. The

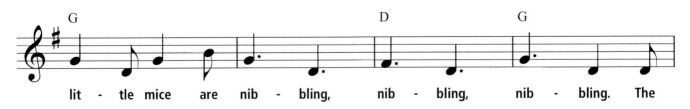

lit - tle mice are nib - bling, nib - bling, nib - bling. The

The Old Gray Cat

lit - tle mice are nib - bling in the house. ___ The

Dancing quietly, but faster

lit - tle mice are danc - ing, danc - ing, danc - ing. The

lit - tle mice are danc - ing in the house.

Moderately creeping

The

old gray cat is creep - ing, creep - ing, creep - ing. The

old gray cat is creep - ing in the house. The

Presto

lit - tle mice are scamp - 'ring, scamp - 'ring, scamp - 'ring. The

lit - tle mice are scamp - 'ring in the house!

The Old Gray Cat

Play the slow and fast sounds, using your fingers on a barred instrument.

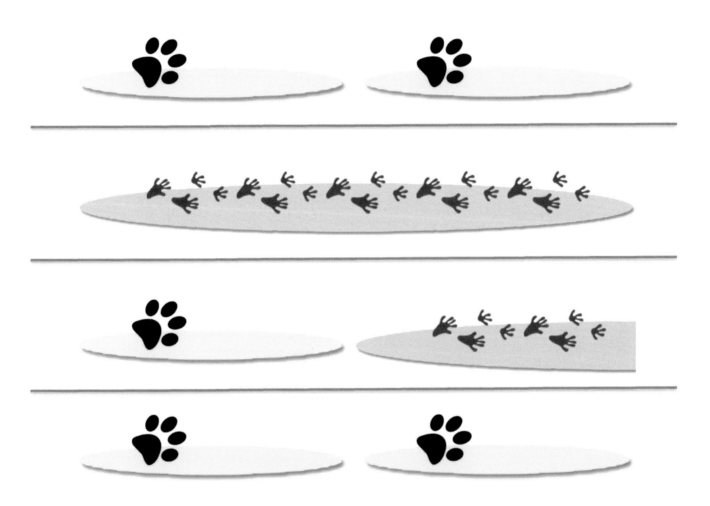

Old MacDonald

Traditional
Arranged by Robert W. Smith

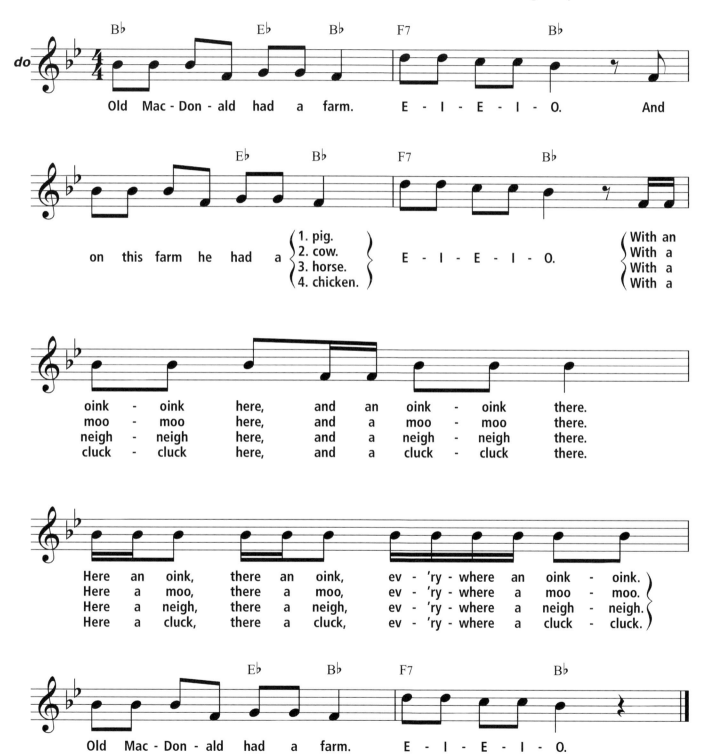

Oliver Twist

Traditional Folk Song of the British Isles and the United States

do

Ol - i - ver Twist, you can't do this,

so what's the use of try - ing?

Touch your knees and touch your toes,

Clap your hands and a - round you go.

On a Log, Mister Frog

Traditional Children's Song of the United States

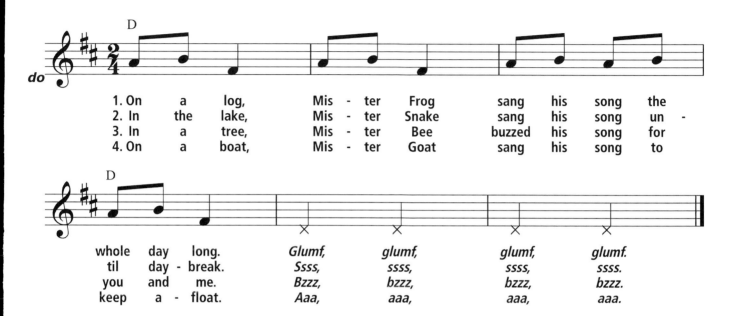

1. On a log, Mis - ter Frog sang his song the
2. In the lake, Mis - ter Snake sang his song un -
3. In a tree, Mis - ter Bee buzzed his song for
4. On a boat, Mis - ter Goat sang his song to

whole day long. *Glumf,* *glumf,* *glumf,* *glumf.*
til day - break. *Ssss,* *ssss,* *ssss,* *ssss.*
you and me. *Bzzz,* *bzzz,* *bzzz,* *bzzz.*
keep a - float. *Aaa,* *aaa,* *aaa,* *aaa.*

Pon, pon, pon
(Tap, Tap, Tap)

Game Song from Mexico
English Words by Bryan Louiselle

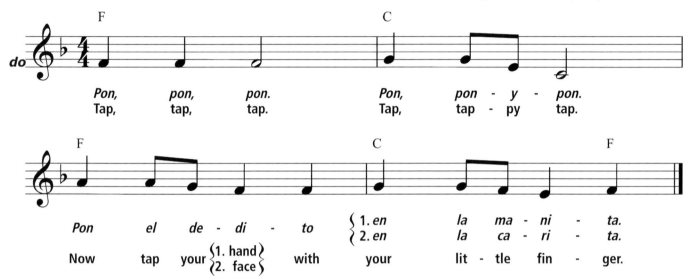

3. ...en la naricita.   3. ...nose...

4. ...en los ojitos.   4. ...eyes...

Put the Beat in Your Feet

Words and Music by
Christine H. Barden

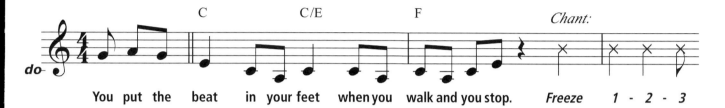

You put the beat in your feet when you walk and you stop. *Freeze* 1 - 2 - 3

You put the beat in your feet when you walk and you stop. *Freeze* 1 - 2 - 3

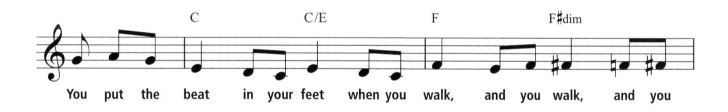

You put the beat in your feet when you walk, and you walk, and you

walk, and walk, and walk, and stop.__ And then you clap your hands.

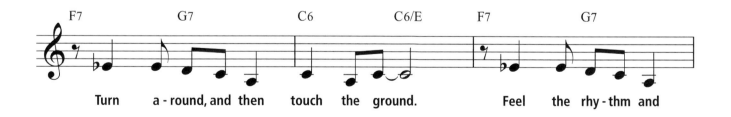

Turn a - round, and then touch the ground. Feel the rhy - thm and

Put the Beat in Your Feet

clap your hands. Then you do a lit-tle hop, hop, hop, hop, hop.

You put the beat in your feet when you walk and you stop. *Freeze 1 - 2 - 3*

You put the beat in your feet when you walk and you stop. *Freeze 1 - 2 - 3*

You put the beat in your feet when you walk, and you walk, and you

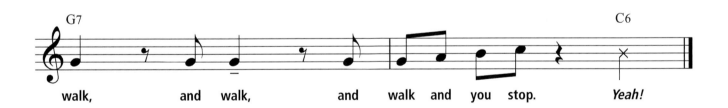

walk, and walk, and walk and you stop. *Yeah!*

Rig-a-Jig-Jig

Folk Song from England

VERSE

do—

1. As   I   was walk - ing
2. As   I   was run - ning
3. As   I   was hop - ping
4. As   I   was skip - ping
} down   the street,   down   the street,   down   the street,

a   nice   young friend   I   chanced   to meet, heigh - o,   heigh-o,   heigh - o.

REFRAIN

Rig - a - jig - jig, and   a - way   we go,   a - way   we go,   a - way   we go;

Rig - a - jig - jig, and   a - way   we go,   heigh - o,   heigh-o, ____ heigh - o.

5. As I was jumping...

6. As I was walking...

Roll Over

Folk Song from the United States

do

There were { ten / nine / eight... } in the bed and the lit-tle one said,

"Roll o - ver, roll o - ver."

1.-8.

So they all rolled o - ver and one fell out. There were

9. *(Last time)*

one fell out, There was one in the bed, and the

lit - tle one said, "Good - night!"

See Saw Pulling Straw

Traditional Melody
Words Adapted by Katherine Brooks
Arranged by Robert W. Smith

Six Little Ducks

Folk Song from Maryland

1. Six lit - tle ducks that I once knew,
2. Down to the riv - er they would go,
3. Home from the riv - er they would come,

Fat ones, skin - ny ones, fair ones, too,
Wibble, wobble, wib - ble, wobble, to and fro,
Wibble, wobble, wib - ble, wobble, ho - hum - hum,

But the one lit - tle duck with a feath - er in his back,

He led the oth - ers with a quack, quack, quack, quack, quack, quack;

He led the oth - ers with a quack, quack, quack, quack, quack, quack.

Tap It! Rap It!

Words and Music by Judith Thomas

Tap it! Rap it!

Find a lit - tle sound. There's mu - sic in the room And there's

mu - sic all a - round. Tap it!

Rap it! Lis - ten to us play,

All the sounds a - round us that we hear each day!

There's No One Exactly Like Me

By Betty Ann Ramseth
Arranged by Robert W. Smith

Happy waltz

Look all the world o - ver, there's no one like

me, no one like me, no one like me. Look

all the world o - ver, there's no one like me. There's

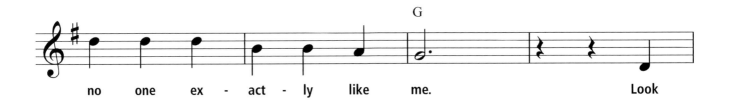

no one ex - act - ly like me. Look

There's No One Exactly Like Me

all   the world   o - ver, there's   no   one   like   you,

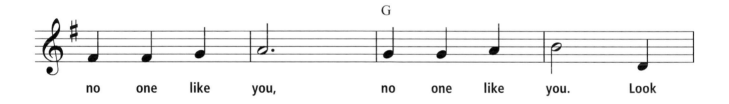

no   one   like   you,   no   one   like   you.   Look

all   the world   o - ver, there's   no   one   like   you.   There's

no   one   ex - act - ly   like   you.

Uga uga uga
(Cake! Cake! Cake!)

Israeli Folk Tune
Hebrew Words by Aharon Ashman
English Words by Susan Greene

U - ga, u - ga, u - ga, Ba - ma a - gal na - chu - ga.
Would you like some cake, cake? Put some on your plate, plate.

Nis - to - ve - va kol - ha o - yam, Ad ash - er nim - tza ma - kom;
Make a cir - cle right a - way, cir - cle 'round so we can play;

La - she - vet la - kum; La - she - vet la - kum; La - she - vet v' - la - kum.
Stand up, now sit down; stand up, now sit down; stand up and now sit down.

We Are Dear Little Birdies

Music by Carl Orff
Words by Judith Thomas

1. We are dear lit - tle bird - ies and the wind blows so cold.
2. We ___ thank you for small things, for ___ crumbs and for seeds.

Will you feed us? Will you feed us? Lit - tle crumbs are like gold.
In the win - ter we are liv - ing, by your gen - er - ous deeds.

When I Grow Up

Music by Carmino Ravosa
Words by Margaret Jones

When I Grow Up

Solo 2: I could feed the an - i - mals down at the zoo,
Solo 4: I could be a pi - lot and fly in the sky, Or
Solo 6: If I were a drum - mer I'd rap-a - tap - tap, Or

D.C. al Coda

rit.

Pea - nuts and pop - corn and lol - li - pops, too.
be a great cook, and make pud-dings and pie.
fly through the air like a great ac - ro - bat.

Coda

rit.   *molto rit.*

I'll try to be an - y - thing that I want to be!

You're Not Ev'rybody

Words and Music by Carmino Ravosa

You're Not Ev'rybody

You're   you,

You're   you,

No - bod - y   else   will   do.

D.C. al Fine